LOCK~DUCKED
PRISON
FOOD
RECIPES

Convict Mac And Cheese

1 chicken Ramen soup
2 pkg. Spam, cubed
1 jalapeño pepper, seeded and diced
1/4 sleeve saltine crackers
1/4 cup salad dressing
1/2 cup squeeze cheese
1/2 tsp. salt
1 tsp. black pepper

In a covered bowl, cook crushed noodles in very hot water for at least half an hour, allowing noodles to absorb as much water as possible. Stir, drain and rinse. Combine the salad dressing, cheese, soup seasoning packet, jalapeño, salt and black pepper with the noodles. Stir continuously until a nice mac & cheese consistency is achieved. Add Spam, stir well. Crush saltines and sprinkle on top of the doodle mixture. Add additional salt, black pepper or hot sauce, if desired.

Flavored Water

1 Ramen packet flavoring your choice of flavor
I cup of warm or hot water cold if you don't have a choice

 Take your cup of water add the ramen flavor pack of your choice, stir, drink, enjoy!

Bail Me Burrito

1 bag refried beans
3 Pouches chili/no beans
2 pouches pot roast
2 packets chili soup seasoning
2 bags pork skins
1 bag cheese puffs
1 bottle squeeze cheese
3 jalapeno peppers
1 can hot V-8 juice
1 bag Salsa Verde chips
1 package tortillas

First, add the beans with the pot roast and 2 chili pouches and mash thoroughly. Add the V-8, chili soup seasoning and 1/2 of the bottle of squeeze cheese, mixing well. Add hot water and mix until consistency is soupy. Crush the pork skins and salsa Verde chips and stir into the mix, adding hot water to keep it slightly soupy. Dice the jalapeños and stir into the mixture. Crush the cheese puffs and add to the mixture, using a little hot water to make it into dough. Spoon the mixture into tortillas and roll until slightly closed, then put rolled burritos into chip bag. Submerge the bag in a hot pot and cook for 2-3 hours. When ready to serve, heat remaining chili pouch and stir in the remaining bottle of squeeze cheese. Pour over the top of burritos.

Tuna Ramen Surprise

1 Package Ramen
1 Slice of American cheese
1 Can of tuna
Jalapeños from the jar

Break up the noodles in the package and cook per the directions. While the noodles are cooking, drain the tuna and dump it into a bowl. Put in the jalapeño slices and top it all off with the slice of cheese. When the Ramen is ready, mix in the spice packet and pour the noodles into the bowl. Let it all steep for a few minutes to melt the cheese and then mix well.

Chili Custody Nachos

1 or 2 packages Chicken chili
1 bag refried beans
1 bag Salsa Verde chips, crushed
1 bottle squeeze cheese
1 bag tortilla chips

Heat chicken chili pouch in hot pot. In a bowl, prepare refried beans to desired thickness. Pour tortilla chips into separate bowl for bottom layer. Mix in chicken-chili and crushed Salsa Verde chips into refried beans, and pour mixture over tortilla chips. Squeeze cheese over bean-chip-chili mixture. Prepare for the heartburn.

Prison Pad Thai
Number 1

One Chicken Ramen package
Tablespoon of Franks red hot sauce
Two Tablespoons of Peanut butter

Cook your ramen, keep about 1/4 cup of water in after you drain it. Next, put the peanut butter in the bottom of your bowl and spread it around. Then put the Franks red hot in add the ramen on top. Mix it all together!

Pen Pad Thai 2

Ramen noodles – 1 package
Peanut butter – 1/3 cup
Crushed peanuts – ¼ cup
Hot sauce – 2 teaspoons

Follow the package instructions and prepare ramen
noodles.
Take a single container and stir all ingredients in it
Use some crushed peanuts to create some crunch.

COUNTY
RAMEN

1 package Ramen noodles and flavor pack
2 packets of mayo
1 packet of mackerel in oil
1-2 hard boiled eggs
2 slices of bread or a tortilla

Heat up your Ramen noodles and drain liquid. Stir in the mayo and flavor pack to taste.Add in the eggs, and mash with fork spoon till crumbled. Stir in whole mackerel package (including oil). If desired, you can combine the dish with bread or a tort to make a finger food meal.

Pokey Pepperoni Pizza

Saltine cracker – 2 sleeves
Tomato Paste
Pepperoni slices
Ritz cracker – 2 sleeves
Onions
Empty plastic bags
Pickles
Ramen noodles – 1 pack
Slim Jim – 1 stick
Block cheese or Squeeze
Cheese

Make thin slices of the pickles, block cheese, onions, and the slim jim.

Take a Dorito bag and combine the two sleeves of Ritz crackers and Saltine crackers in it.

Put the ramen noodles inside the bag after crushing them wholly.

Pour some warm water in the bag. Check if the water matches the level of the mixture.

In order to incorporate the ingredients, mash the blend together for 15 minutes, and cook the noodles.

Once the combination resembles dough, carefully cut the side of the bag and flatten it. Keep another chip bag and to distribute it evenly make use of round material like rolling pin.

Keep the dough to microwave for five minutes.
Roll out the tomato paste in an even manner and mix all the toppings.
Cook the pizza in a microwave for five minutes.

Inmate Mix

One Ramen package Any flavor
Can of Hormel Chili or any kind of chili
Small package of Fritos or any corn chip
Cheese

Boil Noodles to desired state. Drain almost all of noodles except about 1/4 of the water. Place the noodles in a bowl and mix in the seasoning packet, a can of chili, fritos or corn chips, and cheese.

Big House Burrito

Spicy ramen noodles – 1 package
Spicy Jalapeño ranch-flavored popcorn
Squeezable cheese – ¼ cup
Spicy Takis
Tortilla
Cheetos – ½ bag
Crushed cheese-flavored crackers
Any hot sauce

Before opening the pack, crush the whole ramen noodles.
Pour hot water in the bag and cook ramen noodles.
Make sure to tightly close the bag.
Prepare the burrito stuffing while the ramen is cooking.
Merge up the jalapeño popcorn with ramen seasoning.
Afterward, add the crushed cheese crackers, hot sauce, crushed Takis, squeezable cheese.
Take a plastic popcorn bag and mix all ingredients and put on cooked ramen noodles.
Roll out the left over cheese on tortilla.
Put your choice of stuffing and afterwards wrap it.

Prison Pasta

1 Package of Ramen Noodle Soup
 2 cups Tomato Juice
 Add whatever topping looks good such as your
favorite cheese

Add tomato juice to Ramen Noodles along with
seasoning that comes with noodles and cook in
microwave for 2 minutes. Let stand for 1 minute. Cook
a little longer if you like softer noodles.

Reformatory Rice

½ diced onion
½ diced bell pepper
8 Oz diced beef summer sausage
Gochujang or Sriracha Hot Sauce
2 teaspoons minced garlic
1 pack Goya Sazon Con Culantro y Achiote
1-2 tablespoons lime Juice
 2 cups cooked rice
Sweet Asian Chili Sauce
1 ear sweet corn, taken off the cob
¼ cup diced green olives
¼ cup spicy dill pickles, diced
½ cup monterey jack cheese

Fry the onion in the microwave along with summer
sausage for 3-5 minutes on high stir it halfway.
Follow package directions, microwave the pre-cooked
rice separately. Mix goya seasoning and garlic salt.
Take seasoned rice and stir onions and sausages in it
Pour some pickles, peppers, olives, corn, and cheese..

Ramen Trail Mix

1 pack of chili flavor ramen
1/2 cup of raisins
1 cup of peanuts
1/2 cup pitted dates
1/2 cup of dried bananas

Crush the ramen in the wrapper. Add half of the seasoning. Add the dates, raisins, and banana chips. Mix and eat!

Detained Deviled Eggs

Boiled eggs
Sandwich spread
Chili soup seasoning packet

Shell boiled eggs. Cut eggs long ways and remove yolks in a bowl and add sandwich spread. Mix until it becomes a paste. Using a spoon, scoop mixture into egg halves. Lightly garnish by sprinkling chili soup seasoning over the top. Eat and enjoy!

Prison Banana Pudding

6-10 bananas
5 Tbsp white sugar
5 Tbsp non dairy creamer
1 to 3 c hot water.
1 box vanilla wafers cookies

Mix all the contents except the cookie and bananas in a bowl and microwave to boil. When you have it to the consistency you like let pudding cool to room temperature. Layer a bowl with vanilla wafers then bananas and cover with pudding. Keep layering until pudding is gone. Layer a bowl with vanilla wafers then bananas and cover with pudding. Keep layering until pudding is gone.

Manumit Menudo

1 cup tortilla chips
1/4 bag of cooked rice
1 summer sausage or 2 Spams chopped
1 chili/no beans
3 bags pork skins
2 packs of chili seasoning
1/2 pickle chopped with juice

Crush tortilla chips into bowl and add 1/4 cup hot water. Knead into dough. Add cooked rice to the dough and knead. Put content in a bag and heat in hot pot for 10 minutes. In a bowl, combine the summer sausage, the 2 chili soup seasonings, the chili pouch and 1 cup of hot water. In separate bowl add the 3 bags of pork skins and add about a cup of hot water until skins are soft. Mix both bowls together evenly. Add the pickle and juice, combine with the rice mixture.

Slop

2-3 packages of Hot Chili flavored Ramen Noodles
1-2 cans of basic chili or kidney beans.
2-3 cups of rice
1 pkg of flour tortillas
1 can of refried beans
1-2 tomatoes
lettuce
1 small can of black olives
hot sauce

Start boiling water for the ramen noodles and rice (both in different pots). Once that boils put the ramen noodle pkgs in it and cook them and the same with the rice. Once the ramen noodles are done, drain the water out of them and put in the chili or kidney beans (which ever one you like best.) Put the rice in the pot with the ramen noodles and the chili or kidney beans. Once all of this is done, cook your flour tortillas, and put some of the slop onto the tortilla, then follow through as if you were making a taco!

Sweet Slammer Spread

1 Pack duplex cookies
1/2 Pack Regal Graham cookies
15 packs cream cheese
1/3 cup powdered milk
1/3 cup hot chocolate mix
1/3 cup water

Split duplex into halves and set aside in a bowl. In a separate bowl, mix cream cheese, powdered milk, hot chocolate mix and water, stirring into a smooth batter. Crunch Regal Grahams into little chunks over the batter, mix thoroughly. To serve, spread 1/2 spoonfuls onto duplex cookie halves! Best with The Locked Up Latte or Coffee!

Wet Burrito

1 Can of chicken drained save lid
2 tortillas
1 styrafoam cup
1 pitcher of hot water
1 package of ramen any flavor remove seasoning packet
1 small bag of pork rinds
2 small bags of hot cheetohs or dorritos your choice
1 tablespoon roughly of housin sauce
1-2 squirts of sriracha
1/4 cup of dehyrdrated refried beans
1-2 pinches of banana peppers and juice
1/3 of a beef salami log
1 heaping spoonful of nacho cheese
1 plastic tupperware bowl with the lid

Start by taking your styrofoam cup and place ingit before you. Next you will need to put one tortilla in the cup making a C shape inside the cup. Next take the other tortilla and put it in a backwards C shape so all the edges inside the cup of tortilla lined. Open the can of chicken drain the liquid save the lid fore a knife. Use the lid of the tupperware as a cutting board and the chicken can lid as a knife. A paper towel folded up can help you hold the lid to cut with. Chop the chicken up and dump into the plastic bowl. Take the ramen crush in the package and dump into the mix leave out the seasoning packet. Now dump the bag of pork rinds in the mix. Now crush and add one small bag of chips of your choice into the mix.

Add a spoonful of Hoisin sauce into the mix. Now pour in the refried beans. Next add a few banana pepper slices and a squirt of sriracha. Take your 1/3 of a salami roll and chop it up into bite size pieces on your cutting board with your knife. Place the lid on the bowl and shake it up to mix. Spoon the mix into the tortilla lined cup almost to the top. Pour hot water inside the cup to the top of the mix. Tie the plastic bag off and wait 3-5 minutes. Remove bag lay on it's side tear open the bag leaving some underneath to act as a plate. Spread a spoonful of nacho cheese on top like frosting. Add last bag of crumbled chips of your choice on top. Add a few more slices of banana peppers and drizzle sriracha on top. If you like pour a little of the banana pepper juice over the whole thing. Bless your food and eat!

Convict Candy

10 Chick-O-Sticks
3 Milky Way candy bars (melted)
1 bag of Butterfinger Cookies
(crushed)

Crush Chick-O-Sticks and cookies in a large bowl. Melt candy bars in insert cup, pour melted candy bars into bowl with Chick-O-Sticks and cookies, mixing well. Place 1/2 spoonful scoops on flattened chip bag. Let sit for one hour, makes up to 50 pieces of candy or more.

Peanut Butter
Parole Balls

1/2 cup cocoa
2 scoops peanut butter
7 chocolate chip cookies, finely crushed
Several spoonfuls of water
Bag of M&Ms finely crushed
5 vanilla wafers, finely crushed

Mix all ingredients (except crushed vanilla wafers) together until the mixture no longer sticks to the bowl. Take thick mixture and roll into quarter size balls. Take four or five vanilla wafers finely crunched, roll ball and wafer dough together.

Rice noodle Bean Bowl

1 bag of cheetos
1 bag of potato chips
1/4 package of dehydrated refried beans (2-3 oz.)
1 package of rice
1/2 a pickle
1 heaping spoonful of nacho cheese
1/4 a roll of salami diced
1/2 a package of creamy chicken ramen

Place all of the chips and half a package of ramen plus half a seasoning packet in a big back crush and mix. Next take your pickle and salami and dice them up. Pour almost all of the chip mix into a plastic bowl add the diced salami, pickle, refried beans, and rice. Pour hot water over the mix just don't make it soupy. Put the lid on and wait 15 minutes. Now remove lid add some nacho cheese on top. Sprinkle some crushed chips and pickle slices on top. Eat enjoy!

Bunker Brownies

1 pack vanilla wafers or double fudge cookies
1 pack butterscotch candies
2-3 cups hot cocoa

Crush all the cookies in a bowl. In a separate container crush the candies. Take 1/2 of the candy and mix it with the crushed cookies. Mix 1 1/2 to 2 1/2 cups of cocoa in a cup and add a little hot water. Stir it into a glaze. Press the dough mixture flat into the bowl and pour the glaze over it. Serve and enjoy!

Bombay Drink

1 Packet of Instant Coffee
1 Packet of Hawaiian Punch powder
1 Cola

Take both powdered packets and pour into a bowl. Add one tiny splash of cola just enough to wet the powder. Stir the mixture until you cannot stir anymore. Take a cup of ice and spoon the mixture over the ice in the cup. Now slowly pour the cola on top until it reaches the top of the cup. Drink it and you will stay awake FOREVER!

Strawberry Sentence Cheesecake

1 pt. strawberry ice cream, melted
2 packages. Cream cheese
5 banana moon pies
1 packet Instant milk
1 Snickers bar (regular or with almonds)
3/4 package Duplex cookies, crushed (leave in the cream filling)
2 Oatmeal pies, crumbled
5 tbsp. Water

Combine melted ice cream and cream cheese; mix well. Add powdered milk and stir until thick. Melt Snickers in a hot pot, stir into ice cream mixture. In a separate bowl, mix crushed cookies and the crumbled oatmeal pies. Add water gradually until you can mold the mixture into a crust inside the bowl. Add ice cream mixture and let sit for at least four hours. Enjoy! This recipe works well with chocolate ice cream, too.

Sweetest Thang In Prison

1 Honey Bun
1-2 Tablespoons of peanut butter
1 cosmic brownie broken in half
1 package of reeses peanut butter cups
1 snickers bar broken in half

Take your honey bun and open it up spread the peanut butter on top of it. Take half of a cosmic brownie and place it on top of the peanut butter. Add one reeses cup on top of that. Now add a half snickers bar on top. Place in the microwave for 10 seconds! Eat and enjoy!

Outlaw Oatmeal

3/4 cup of rehydrated milk
1 1/2 packages oatmeal-
regular flavor
3 tbsp. melted peanut butter
1 sweetener
1/2 Butterfinger candy bar

Cool oatmeal with hot water, making it thick. Pour into cup and add milk, melt peanut butter and add to oatmeal stirring in one sweetener. Last, add a crushed Butterfinger on top of the light, milky peanut butter oatmeal.

Cellblock Salsa

1 V-8 Vegetable Juice
3 jalapeno peppers, diced
1 chili soup seasoning pack
1 cup jalapeño potato chips,
finely crushed
1 tsp. black pepper

Mix all ingredients and enjoy! Works well as a dip, on nachos or in burritos.

Orange Liberation
Cheese Cake

Sugar – 1 packet
French vanilla creamer – 2 tablespoons
Kool-Aid (any flavor) – ¾ cup
Cookies (any kind) – 12 Oz
Cream cheese – 6 Oz
Honey – 2 tablespoons

Make a mixture of all the cookies. Until you get sweet crumbs, crush the whole cookies.
Cook the crushed cookies in a microwave for 3-4 minutes. Allow them to cool down.
Take a bowl and mix the sugar, French vanilla creamer, cream cheese, honey, and Kool-Aid.
Fill up the top of the crushed cookie crust by the mixture. Roll out the frosting at uniform level.
Take an ice-filled bucket and refrigerate it for 4-5 hours or unless the toppings get solid.

Pinch Pie

Sugar Packets
Honey Packets
Graham Crackers
Canned Yams
Butter Packets – (5-6
pieces)

Crush all the graham crackers and keep them in the separate container.

Defrost the butter and stream it into meshed graham crackers.

Push the crushed graham on a flat surface until it looks like a "crust."

Push the canned yams for the filling and mix honey, sugar, and butter.

On the top of crushed graham crackers spread the blend in even manner.

Keep the pie to get baked for 25 minutes.

Slice the pie and taste it!

Chocolate Chip
Confinement Cake

Chips Ahoy – 1 pack
Oreos – 1 pack
Milk – 1 carton
Mayo – 1 container

Mash the Oreos and Chips Ahoy cookies.
Take a bowl and keep all crushed cookies. Continue
mashing cooking unless you get a fine mixture.
Take the carton of milk and heat it, and stream it in the
mix.
Pour some mayo in the blend. This keeps the
combination together.
Keep it to microwave for 3-5 minutes

Prison Bar Butterscotch Brownies

Vanilla wafers (or double fudge cookies) – 1 pack
Butterscotch candies – 1 whole bag
Hot cocoa powder – 2 cups

Take a container and crush the wafers and cookies.
Crush the butterscotch candies in the separate bag
Blend the both crushed mixtures.
Mix some small amounts of warm water to your cocoa powder.
Into a flat surface, push the blend of cookies and candies.
On the top of the crust, stream some cocoa powder like a glaze.

Locked Up Latte

A small carton of milk
Instant coffee – 3 tablespoons
Maple syrup packet – 1

Unless the milk is steamy, in hot water, run the small
milk carton. (Via tap or via boiling)
Take a separate container and stream the milk in it.
Stream the instant coffee along with maple syrup.
Stir it wholly, and enjoy your drink!

Trammel Tamale

Meat stick or beef jerky
sausage – 1 Oz
Warm water – ½ cup
Corn chips – 1 large bag
Cheese curls or processed
cheese food – 1/3 cup

Amalgamate the corn chips and cheese in the one chip bag.
Make the fine blend by crushing.
Cut the meat stick properly and add it up with a blend.
To make it shape it to a tamale, stream some water in the mixture.
Keep the bag under hot water to cook after closing the bag tightly.
Enjoy the taste of your tamales.

Restrain Me Ramen

Ramen Noodles
Doritos (or Cheez-Its)
Jack Mack or Canned
Tuna
Hot Sauce

Wholly cook the ramen noodles.
Also, mash the Doritos or Cheez-Its
Add up the crush cheese snacks when you are done
with ramen noodles. It shall resemble like made-up
cheese sauce.
You can serve it along with the extra hot sauce, Jack
Mack, or Tuna toppings.

Captured Chi Chi

Butter
Hot Sauce
Precooked can/package of chili
Cayenne pepper
A pack of Ramen noodles
Canned sausages
Salt and Pepper
Onion and Garlic powder

Take a bowl and boil some water in it. Use the hot water for cooking ramen noodles.
Keep some butter to melt.
Add the hot sauce, garlic powder, cayenne pepper, salt, pepper, onion in the melted butter. Blend it nicely.
Add up the sliced canned sausages to the pre-cooked chili.
Mix the pre-made butter mixture with the chili and sausage mixture and Keep to heat up in the microwave the complete mix.
Pour all the ramen noodles in sauce.

Lockup Loaf

Ramen noodles chili – 1 package
Cheetos (1.25 oz.) – 1 bag
Slightly less than half a tumbler of the warmest water available
Saved meat
Many variations of this recipe include jalapeño chips, Flaming Hot Cheetos, basically anything which is available in your canteen commissary.

You can keep the left-over meat or cheese from your food trays in a plastic bag.
To get the flavor package out, open the bags of ramen noodles slightly.
Gently break the noodle brick apart inside the bag; be careful not to lose any.
To discard the air and smash those apart, open up the bag of Cheetos slightly.
Make small bits out of meat.
Open the top flap of Cheetos completely. Shift the noodle bits, mix some meat, stream seasoning, and shake it for a minute to get a proper blend.
Stream some water, and discard all air from the bag, fold it up.
Use a towel to wrap it and let it rest for 10 minutes.
Discard from towel oven and open the bag in the middle.

Pound Porkies

Cooked rice
Kool-aid – 3 tablespoons
Ramen noodles
Pork rinds

First, nicely mash all the ramen noodles and soak it in hot water in a bowl.
Stream three tablespoons of Kool-Aid in three separate containers.
Pour some hot water of 1 tablespoon in the powder and mix it wholly to create sauce out of it.
Mix the pork rinds and Coat up all the pork rinds pieces with the sauce.
Keep the skins to the microwave for five minutes.
Mix the cooked rice with strained ramen noodles.
Create some appeal by keeping pork rinds on the top of the ramen along with the cooked rice.

Chocolate Dipped Chips

2 bars of Hershey's chocolate
1-2 bags of Ruffles potato chips

Put the two unopened hershey bars into a container of hot water. Let them sit for a minute until they are melted. Pour the chocolate into a bowl. Now dip one side of a potato chip then set it on a plate. Repeat the process until all the chip or chocolate are gone. Eat and enjoy!

Convict Chinese
Take Out

I heaping spoonful of peanut butter
1 packet of soy sauce
1 spoon of smuggled garlic if you can get some
1 package of beef ramen
1 piece of chicken stolen from your dinner tray
1 green bean stolen from your dinner tray
1 piece of bell pepper stolen from your dinner tray
1 scoop of cooked rice
1 scoop of jalapenos
1 scoop of crushed peanuts for topping

Put the peanut butter in a bowl pour the soy sauce on top add garlic if you have it. Stir until well bleded then set aside. Cook ramen noodles then drain alost all the water add half the packet of seasoning. Stir until mixed. Chop up the chicken, pepper, and green bean using your ID card. Stir the peanut butter mixture into the noodles. Add the rice, and chopped pieces. Place some jalapenos in the mix too. Stir everything then top with the peanuts. Eat and enjoy!

Your Recipe:

Ingredients:

Directions:

Your Recipe:

Ingredients:

_____

_____

_____

_____

_____

_____

_____

Directions:

_____

_____

_____

_____

_____

_____

_____

_____

_____

_____

Your Recipe:

Ingredients:

_____

_____

_____

_____

_____

_____

_____

Directions:

_____

_____

_____

_____

_____

_____

_____

_____

_____

_____

Your Recipe:

Ingredients:

_____

_____

_____

_____

_____

_____

_____

Directions:

_____

_____

_____

_____

_____

_____

_____

_____

_____

Your Recipe:

Ingredients:

Directions:

Your Recipe:

Ingredients:

Directions:

Your Recipe:

Ingredients:

Directions:

Your Recipe:

Ingredients:

Directions:

Your Recipe:

Ingredients:

_____

_____

_____

_____

_____

_____

_____

_____

Directions:

_____

_____

_____

_____

_____

_____

_____

_____

_____

_____

Your Recipe:

Ingredients:

Directions:

Made in the USA
Columbia, SC
16 October 2024